The MAIASAURA NESTS

Jack Horner's Dinosaur Eggs

by Duncan Searl

Consultant: Jack Horner
Curator of Paleontology
Museum of the Rockies
Bozeman, Montana

 HOUGHTON MIFFLIN   BOSTON

Credits

Cover, © Syracuse Newspaper / John Berry / The Image Works; Title Page, © AP Wide World Photos; 4, © Museum of the Rockies, Bozeman, Montana; 5, © Karen Carr; 6, © Museum of the Rockies, Bozeman, Montana; 9, © Museum of the Rockies, Bozeman, Montana; 10, © Michael S. Yamashita/Corbis; 11, © Louie Psihoyos / Science Faction; 12, © Dorling Kindersley Media Library; 13T, © Louie Psihoyos / Science Faction; 13B, © Museum of the Rockies, Bozeman, Montana; 14, © age/foto stock/ SuperStock; 15T, © Louie Psihoyos / Science Faction; 15B, © Laurie O'Keefe / Photo Researchers, Inc.; 16, © Museum of the Rockies, Bozeman, Montana; 17, © Phillippe Hays / Peter Arnold, Inc.; 18, © Bennett Darrel/ Animals Animals-Earth Scenes; 19, © Earnest Manewal / SuperStock; 20–21, © Jack Novak / SuperStock; 22, © SuperStock; 23, © Charlie McGrady Studio; 24, © Museum of the Rockies, Bozeman, Montana; 25, © Museum of the Rockies, Bozeman, Montana; 26, © Museum of the Rockies, Bozeman, Montana; 27, © Louie Psihoyos / Science Faction; 28–29 Rodica Prato; 28, © Dorling Kindersley; 29T, © Joe Tucciarone; 29B, © Natural History Museum Picture Library, London.

Table of Contents

A Rock Shop Surprise

Jack Horner wandered through a tiny Montana rock shop. It was cluttered with dusty rocks and **fossils** for sale.

The owner, Marion Brandvold, knew that Jack was a fossil hunter. He was an expert at identifying dinosaur bones. She showed him some fossils she had found.

Jack Horner

Jack stared at one of the gray bones. He couldn't believe his eyes. The owner had the jawbone of a baby duck-billed dinosaur.

At that time, in 1978, hardly any fossils of dinosaur babies had been found. So scientists knew next to nothing about the lives of young dinosaurs. Jack had to find out where Marion's fossils had come from.

A duck-billed dinosaur was a large plant-eating dinosaur with a duck-like beak. Many types of duckbills once lived in North America.

An artist's rendering of duck-billed dinosaurs.

The Salad Bowl

Jack drove with Marion to a nearby cattle ranch. She showed him the **mound** of **mudstone** where she'd found the bones. Some fossil bits were lying on top.

Jack dug into the mound. He found that the mudstone filled a large hole in the surrounding rock. The hole measured six feet (2 m) across and three feet (1 m) deep. To Jack, it looked like a giant stone salad bowl.

Jack searched for baby dinosaur fossils in this area in northwest Montana.

Over the next few days, Jack studied the mudstone from inside the bowl. He found that it held the bones of 15 baby dinosaurs.

News of the discovery spread quickly. Jack Horner had dug up a dinosaur nest!

The Fossils in the Nest

About 70 million years ago, a dinosaur made a mound of dirt and then dug out the center as a nest for her eggs. Later, mud filled in the nest and turned into stone. The baby dinosaurs inside turned into fossils.

Jack dug out big chunks of mudstone from the dinosaur nest. He then used water from a hose to separate the fossils from the dirt and mudstone.

Growing Up Among Fossils

Fossils had long been a part of Jack Horner's life. Jack grew up in northwestern Montana, an area famous for fossils. When he was eight years old, Jack found his first dinosaur bone.

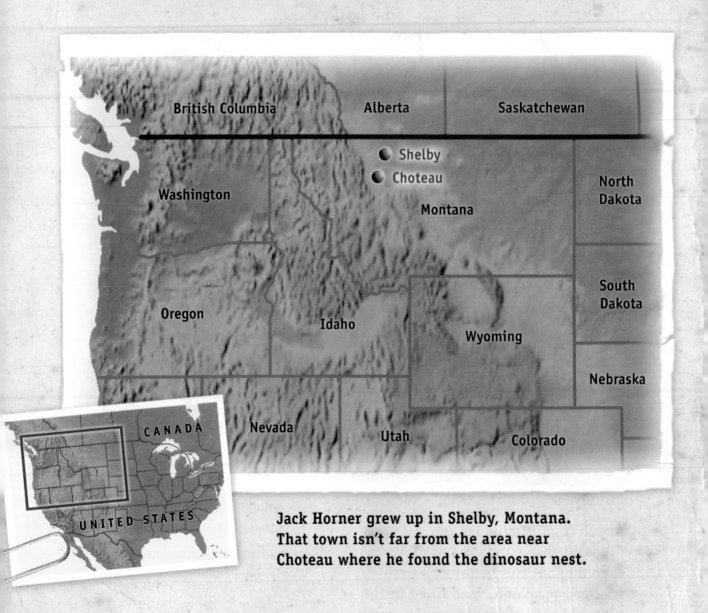

Jack Horner grew up in Shelby, Montana. That town isn't far from the area near Choteau where he found the dinosaur nest.

Jack's favorite subject was science. For a science project, he once launched a homemade rocket 15,000 feet (4,572 m) high! Young Jack struggled in most of his other subjects, though. Reading was especially hard.

No one knew it, but Jack suffered from **dyslexia**. Sometimes he struggled over a word for half an hour. When Jack graduated from high school, he only had a D average. A career in **paleontology** seemed unlikely.

Jack in the Cub Scouts

A Rocky Road

Jack Horner went to college, but dyslexia made it very difficult, so he went to work running his family's gravel business. Jack still loved dinosaurs, though. He kept reading about fossils—and kept finding them, too.

Jack knew so much about dinosaurs that in 1975 he finally got a job at Princeton University in New Jersey. He worked there as a museum **preparator**. It was hard, dusty work, chipping fossils out of chunks of stone.

This preparator cleans the fossils of an *Albertosaurus*.

During his vacation in the summer of 1978, Jack went back to Montana. He knew that the fossils of young dinosaurs had been found there. Perhaps he'd get lucky and find some, too.

Preparators putting fossils together

Preparators often help at fossil-hunting expeditions during the summer. The rest of the year, they clean the fossils and put the bones together into dinosaur displays.

More Discoveries

While Jack was in Montana, he heard about Marion and her rock shop. He knew she wanted help identifying fossils. So he stopped by to take a look. What he didn't know was that she would lead him to a nest of dinosaur babies—and that was just the beginning!

This model shows what one of the dinosaur's nests may have looked like millions of years ago.

Between 1978 and 1983, Jack Horner and his team searched the area near the first nest. They uncovered 13 more dinosaur nests. In them, they found many more duck-billed baby bones. They also found eggs and broken bits of eggshells.

Jack and his crew lived in Native American-style tepees during their search for fossils.

Some of the first dinosaur eggs were discovered in Mongolia in 1923. Before then, scientists thought that dinosaurs laid eggs, but they had no proof.

Looking at All the Clues

Paleontologists don't just dig up fossils. They also use the fossils to draw conclusions. Jack noticed the nests he found were exactly 23 feet (7 m) apart. What did this mean?

Jack thought about the way some groups of birds lay out nests on the ground. They often use the length of their outstretched wings to space out their nests.

Flamingos, like many birds, nest in groups called colonies.

Jack connected the spacing of the birds' nests to the spacing of the dinosaur nests. There was just enough room for a mother dinosaur to turn around without bumping into her neighbor. The evenly spaced nests showed Jack that many dinosaurs nested together in one spot.

The adult dinosaurs that made the nests were about 25 feet (8 m) long. They weighed up to 3 tons (2.7 metric tons).

This drawing shows how the dinosaurs that Jack discovered may have made nests in colonies, like birds.

15

Good Mother Lizards

Jack also noticed that the eggshells in many of the nests were crushed. The eggshells were another clue about how the dinosaurs lived.

If the babies had left the nests right away, they wouldn't have had time to **trample** the shells into small pieces. So the babies must have lived in the nests for awhile. In Jack's view, the dinosaur mothers brought food to their babies while they grew up in the nests.

This model shows how the dinosaurs that Jack discovered may have taken care of their babies in the nests.

Jack concluded that the dinosaurs he found had been good mothers. Unlike today's **reptiles**, they had fed and cared for their young. *Maiasaura* (*mye*-uh-SOR-uh), or "good mother lizard," seemed like a perfect name to give them.

Modern-day reptiles, such as the green iguana, do not return to their nests once they lay their eggs.

The baby dinosaurs Jack found were different from any known duck-billed dinosaurs. So they were classified as a new **species**.

Cold-blooded or Warm?

In the past, scientists assumed that dinosaurs were **cold-blooded**, like other reptiles. The *Maiasaura* nests led Jack to think that, instead, dinosaurs might be **warm-blooded**, like birds. How did he reach this conclusion?

Baby reptiles leave their nests to search for food as soon as they hatch. Many baby birds, however, stay in the nest for weeks.

Most kinds of baby birds stay in their nests until they are old enough and strong enough to take care of themselves.

Jack found small skeletons of baby dinosaurs in some of the nests. He found larger baby skeletons in others. Did the difference in size show that the babies spent time growing in the nests? Jack thought that it did. *Maiasaura* babies grew up like birds. So they were probably warm-blooded like them, too.

Reptile babies don't stay in their nests. These baby sea turtles, for example, head for the sea as soon as they hatch.

In some nests the *Maiasaura* babies were only 14 inches (36 cm) long. In other nests they had grown to over 3 feet (1 m).

A Giant Bone Bed

The *Maiasaura* fossils helped Jack understand how the dinosaurs had lived. Yet why did the babies die before leaving their nests? A discovery nearby suggested an answer.

In a strip of land about one mile (1.6 km) wide, Jack uncovered the bones of 10,000 adult maiasaurs. This giant **bone bed** was also full of **volcanic ash**. Eighty million years ago, Montana was a land of many volcanoes. Poisonous gas from a huge **eruption** probably killed the thousands of maiasaurs. Later, a **mudflow** may have swept their bodies together. The same volcanic gas could have killed the babies in the nesting ground.

In modern times, one of North America's largest volcanic eruptions occurred at Mount St. Helens in Washington State. During the age of the dinosaurs, North America's volcanoes were much larger.

The *Maiasaura* bones in the bone bed did not look like they had been chewed. So those maiasaurs had probably not been killed by animals.

Living in Herds

The giant bone bed might have answered one question. Yet it raised another one. Suppose a volcano had killed thousands of maiasaurs. What were all these dinosaurs doing together in the same place? To answer that question, Jack Horner imagined how *Maiasaura* lived.

A bison herd in South Dakota

In his mind, Jack pictured huge **herds** of the dinosaurs on the Montana plains. Perhaps thousands of them roamed the land together as they looked for plants to eat. In some ways, the maiasaurs would have been like herds of modern bison that roam the plains as they **graze** on grass.

Traveling in herds provides some protection from **predators**. A few herd members serve as guards, warning the others when enemies approach.

Predators such as *Daspletosaurus* (dass-*plee*-toh-SOR-uhss) may have hunted the *Maiasaura* herds.

Life in the Herd

Most people think of dinosaurs as **prehistoric** loners. By picturing huge herds of maiasaurs, Jack Horner has challenged another common idea about these ancient creatures. He has also started a new kind of search. He wants to know more about how the maiasaurs lived together.

Jack walks on the bone bed that contained the fossils of 10,000 maiasaurs.

Scientists can't tell the **gender** of the maiasaurs whose fossils were found in the bone bed. So they aren't sure if the *Maiasaura* herds contained mainly males, mainly females, or both.

Did the dinosaurs live in herds all the time, or only for part of the year? How did a male maiasaur attract a mate? How did the maiasaurs defend themselves?

These are some of the questions that Jack has asked. He has lots of others, too. With any luck, the fossils may give him the answers someday.

Jack Horner was an adviser for the dinosaur movie *Jurassic Park,* **and its sequels.**

The Museum of the Rockies

Today, Jack Horner is back home in Montana. As **curator** of the Museum of the Rockies, he is in charge of displaying many of the fossils he has found.

Jack doesn't mount his fossils on steel frames, like most museums do. Instead, he displays bones as the paleontologists found them. That way, visitors to the museum can draw their own conclusions about dinosaurs.

A display of fossils at the Museum of the Rockies

Fortunately, the Museum of the Rockies isn't far from fossil country. So whenever he has the time, Jack Horner heads for the hills to do what he loves most—dig for dinosaurs!

Jack Horner holding a model of a *Maiasaura* baby at the Museum of the Rockies

Maiasaura captured the hearts of people in Montana. In 1985, the state made the "good mother lizard" its official fossil.

A Trip Back in Time: Who Lived with *Maiasaura*?

Dinosaurs lived on Earth for around 150 million years. Scientists divide the time in which the dinosaurs lived into three periods—the Triassic period (250 to 205 million years ago), the Jurassic period (205 to 145 million years ago), and the Cretaceous period (145 to 65 million years ago).

Maiasaura lived near the end of the Cretaceous period. Here are three other dinosaurs that lived at the same time and in the same place as *Maiasaura*.

Albertosaurus

This large, powerful meat-eater preyed on maiasaurs and other duck-billed dinosaurs.

FACTS

Albertosaurus
(al-*bur*-toh-SOR-uhss)

- has a name that means "Alberta lizard," because its bones were first found in Alberta, Canada
- walked on its two hind legs, using its long tail to help keep its balance
- had long jaws with about 70 large, saw-like teeth
- **size:** 30 feet (9 m) long and 11 feet (3.3 m) high at the hips

Ornithomimus

Ornithomimus probably ran in and out of the *Maiasaura* herds, searching for insects, fruit, eggs, and small reptiles to eat.

FACTS

Ornithomimus
(or-*nith*-oh-MYE-muhss)

- name means "bird mimic"
- looked similar to an ostrich, with a small head, long neck, and long legs
- could probably run as fast as 40 miles per hour (64 kph)
- **size:** 15–20 feet (4.5–6 m) long and 6–8 feet (1.8–2.4 m) high at the hips

Euoplocephalus

This plant-eater looked for food in the same areas as the maiasaurs. It probably traveled in herds, too.

FACTS

Euoplocephalus
(*yoo*-op-luh-SEF-uh-luhss)

- name means "well-armored head"
- belonged to a group of dinosaurs called ankylosaurs (AN-kee-luh-*sorz*)
- had large horns and thick plates in its skin, which provided good protection from predators
- **size:** 20 feet (6 m) long

Glossary

bone bed (BOHN BED)
a place where many fossils are found

cold-blooded (*kohld*-BLUHD-id)
having blood that changes temperature based on the temperature of the surrounding environment

curator (KYOO-ray-tur)
a person in charge of all or part of a museum or art gallery

dyslexia (diss-LEK-see-uh)
a difficulty in reading because the person may see letters or words in the wrong order

eruption (i-RUP-shun)
the sending out of lava, ash, steam, and gas from a volcano

fossils (FOSS-uhlz)
what is left of plants or animals that lived long ago

gender (JEN-dur)
being male or female

graze (GRAYZ)
eat grass growing on plains or other places

herds (HURDS)
large groups of animals

mound (MOUND)
a pile or small hill

mudflow (MUHD-floh)
a moving mass of mud that is usually caused by heavy rains

mudstone (MUHD-stone)
rock that is formed from layers of mud that have been pressed together for a long period of time

paleontology (*pale*-ee-uhn-TOL-uh-jee)
the study of ancient plants, animals, and rocks

predators (PRED-uh-turz)
animals that hunt other animals for food

prehistoric (*pree*-hi-STOR-ik)
more than 5,500 years ago, which was before the time when people began to use writing to record history

preparator (pri-PAIR-uh-tur)
a person whose job is to prepare and sometimes help find fossils for displays

reptiles (REP-tilez)
cold-blooded animals that usually have dry, scaly skin, such as lizards, snakes, turtles, or crocodiles

species (SPEE-sheez)
groups that animals are divided into, according to similar characteristics; members of the same species can have offspring together

trample (TRAM-puhl)
to crush something by walking on it

volcanic ash (vol-KAN-ik ASH)
tiny pieces of rock and mineral that are sent out by a volcano during an eruption

warm-blooded (*worm*-BLUHD-id)
having blood that stays the same temperature no matter the temperature of the environment

Bibliography

Horner, John R., and Edwin Dobb. *Dinosaur Lives: Unearthing an Evolutionary Saga.* New York: HarperCollins (1997).

Horner, John R., and James Gorman. *Digging Dinosaurs.* New York: Workman Publishing (1998).

Lessem, Don. *Kings of Creation: How a New Breed of Scientists Is Revolutionizing Our Understanding of Dinosaurs.* New York: Simon and Schuster (1992).

Read More

Horner, John R., and Don Lessem. *Digging Up Tyrannosaurus rex.* New York: Crown (1995).

Horner, John R., and James Gorman. *Maia: A Dinosaur Grows Up.* Philadelphia, PA: Running Press (1987).

Psihoyos, Louie, with John Knoebber. *Hunting Dinosaurs.* New York: Random House (1995).

Zoehfeld, Kathleen Weidner. *Dinosaur Parents, Dinosaur Young: Uncovering the Mystery of Dinosaur Families.* New York: Clarion Books (2001).

Index

About the Author

Duncan Searl is a writer and editor who lives in New York. He is the author of many books for young readers.

The
cat
on the
chimney

Solving problems with technology

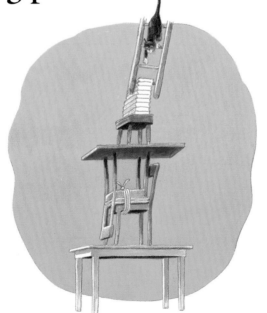

David Drew
Illustrated by Robert Roennfeldt

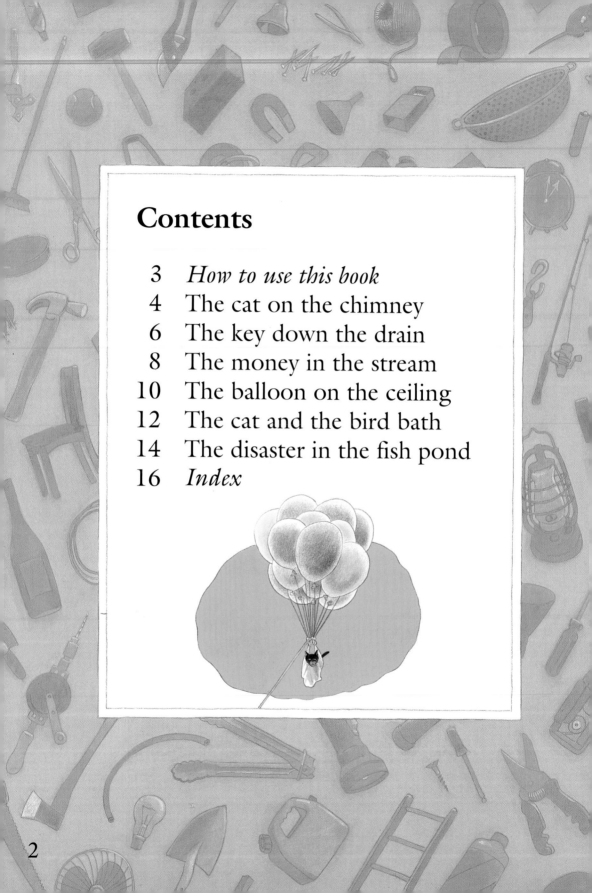

Contents

How to use this book

You can solve all the problems
in this book using technology.
But remember, your solution
must work, it must be safe, and it
should be cheap and easy to make.

   Try to use only the things in the
picture. Add extra things if you
think they will work better. There
are many correct solutions.

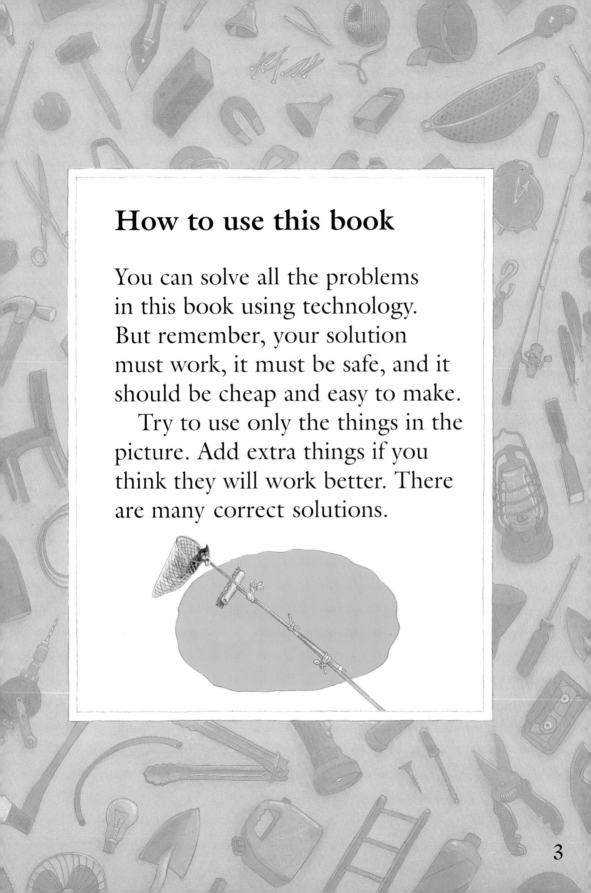

The cat on the chimney

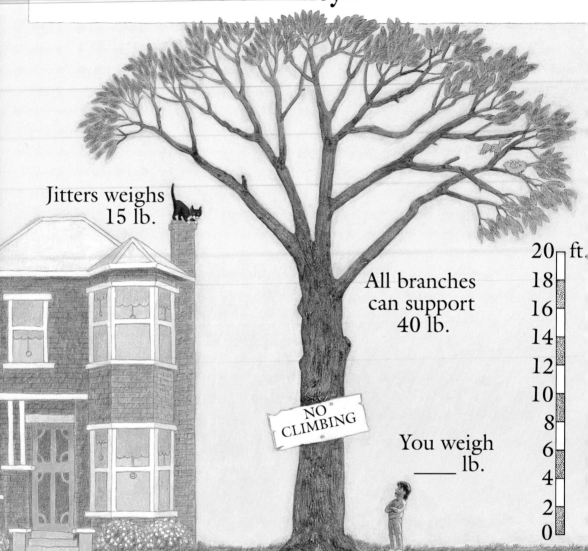

Jitters weighs 15 lb.

All branches can support 40 lb.

NO CLIMBING

You weigh ____ lb.

20 ft.
18
16
14
12
10
8
6
4
2
0

Your cat Jitters is balanced on top of the chimney and is afraid to come down.

How can you rescue him without causing harm or injury?

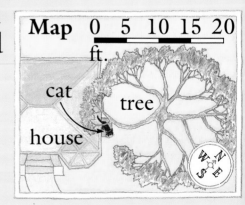

Map   0   5   10 15 20
                           ft.

cat

tree

house

Use one or more of these things:

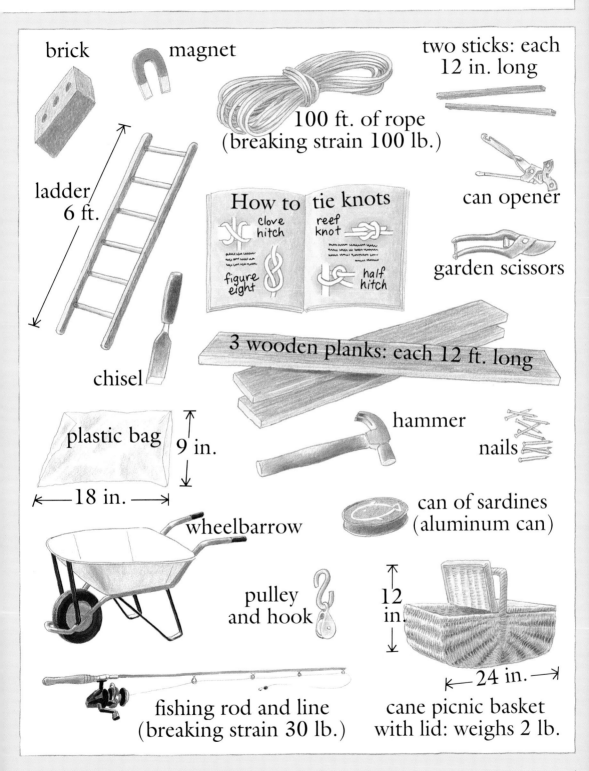

brick

magnet

two sticks: each 12 in. long

100 ft. of rope (breaking strain 100 lb.)

ladder 6 ft.

How to tie knots

clove hitch

reef knot

figure eight

half hitch

can opener

garden scissors

chisel

3 wooden planks: each 12 ft. long

plastic bag — 9 in. — 18 in.

hammer

nails

wheelbarrow

can of sardines (aluminum can)

pulley and hook

12 in.

24 in.

fishing rod and line (breaking strain 30 lb.)

cane picnic basket with lid: weighs 2 lb.

5

The key down the drain

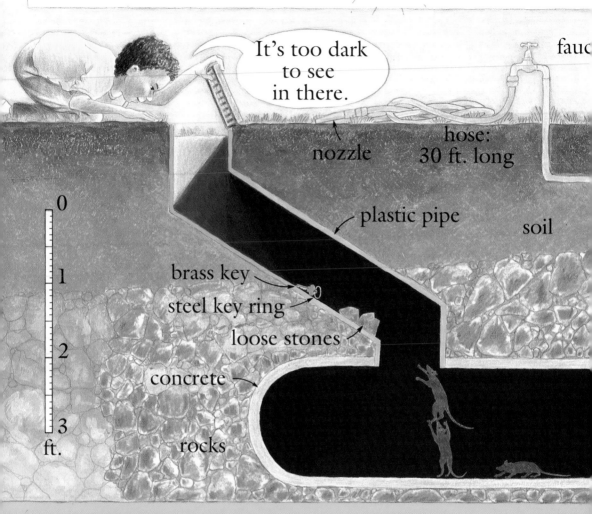

It's too dark to see in there.

nozzle

hose: 30 ft. long

fauc

plastic pipe

soil

brass key

steel key ring

loose stones

concrete

rocks

0
1
2
3
ft.

Your friend, Ernest Dithering, has accidentally dropped your key down the drain.

What do you need to find the key and get the key out?

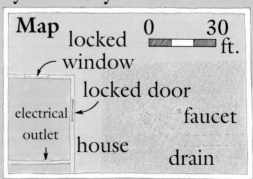

Map locked window

locked door

0 — 30 ft.

electrical outlet

house

faucet

drain

Use one or more of these things:

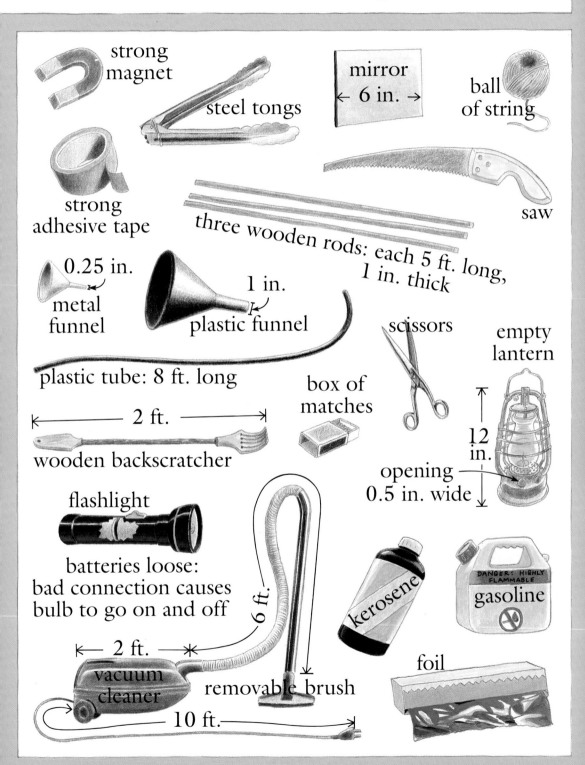

strong magnet

steel tongs

mirror
← 6 in. →

ball of string

strong adhesive tape

three wooden rods: each 5 ft. long, 1 in. thick

saw

0.25 in.

metal funnel

1 in.

plastic funnel

scissors

empty lantern

plastic tube: 8 ft. long

box of matches

12 in.

← 2 ft. →

wooden backscratcher

opening 0.5 in. wide

flashlight

batteries loose: bad connection causes bulb to go on and off

6 ft.

kerosene

DANGER: HIGHLY FLAMMABLE

gasoline

foil

← 2 ft. →

vacuum cleaner

removable brush

← 10 ft. →

The money in the stream

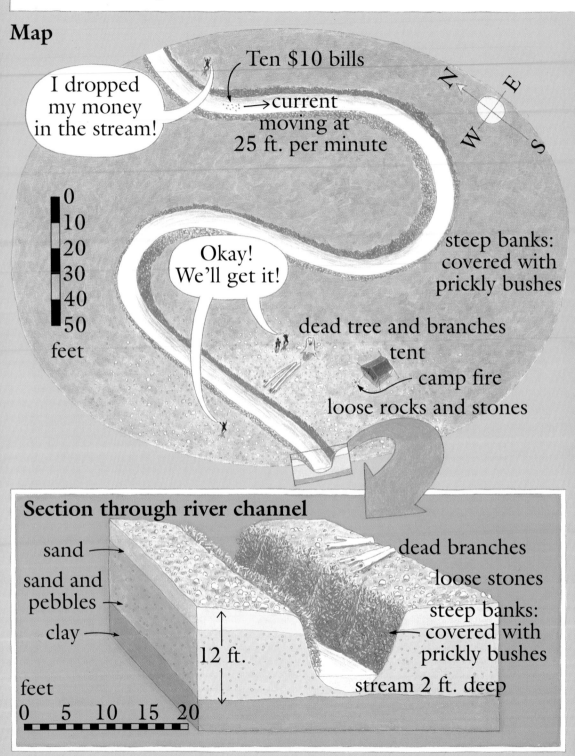

All you have are these things:

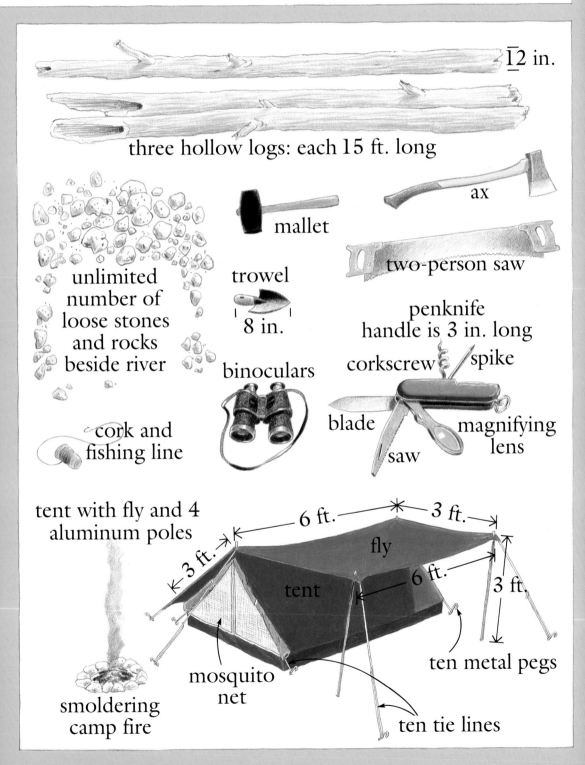

12 in.

three hollow logs: each 15 ft. long

ax

mallet

two-person saw

unlimited number of loose stones and rocks beside river

trowel

8 in.

penknife
handle is 3 in. long

corkscrew   spike

binoculars

blade

saw

magnifying lens

cork and fishing line

tent with fly and 4 aluminum poles

6 ft.   3 ft.

3 ft.

fly

tent

6 ft.

3 ft.

ten metal pegs

mosquito net

smoldering camp fire

ten tie lines

9

The balloon on the ceiling

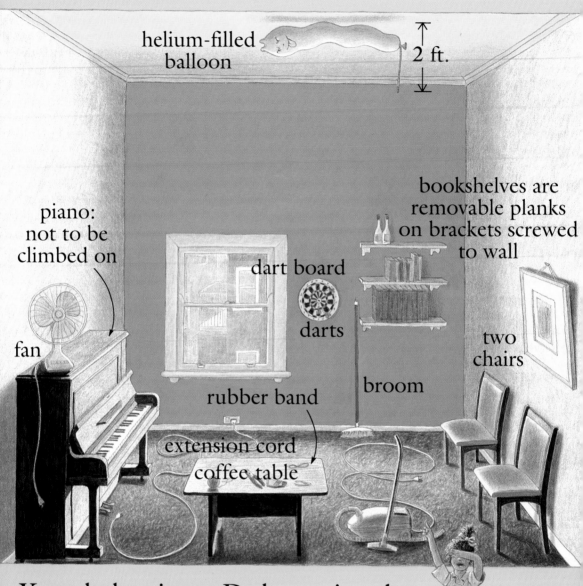

helium-filled balloon

2 ft.

bookshelves are removable planks on brackets screwed to wall

piano: not to be climbed on

dart board

darts

two chairs

fan

rubber band

broom

extension cord

coffee table

Your baby sister, Dolores, just let go her helium-filled balloon.

How can you get it down safely? How can you make sure your sister won't lose it again?

The things in the picture are this big:

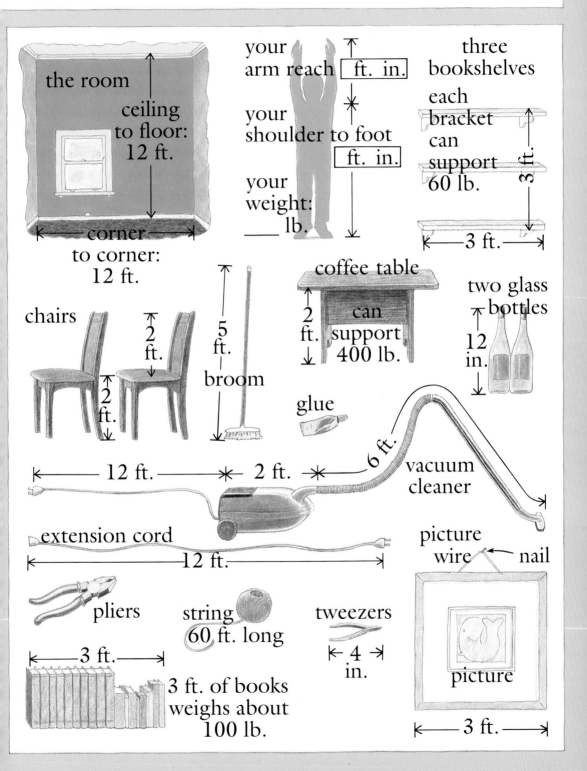

the room

ceiling to floor: 12 ft.

corner to corner: 12 ft.

your arm reach [ft. in.]

your shoulder to foot [ft. in.]

your weight: ___ lb.

three bookshelves each bracket can support 60 lb.

3 ft.

3 ft.

chairs

2 ft.

2 ft.

5 ft.

broom

coffee table

2 ft. can support 400 lb.

two glass bottles

12 in.

glue

6 ft.

vacuum cleaner

12 ft. — 2 ft. — 6 ft.

extension cord

12 ft.

picture wire — nail

pliers

3 ft.

3 ft. of books weighs about 100 lb.

string 60 ft. long

tweezers

4 in.

picture

3 ft.

11

The cat and the bird bath

2 ft. 6 in.

3 ft. high

cat can climb
wooden post
using claws
to hang on

Map

fence: 6 ft. high

door

window
ledge

retractable
clothes line
5 ft. high

window

bird bath
3 ft. high

house

0 1 2 3
ft.

Al Fresco can jump 6 ft.

0   1   2   3   4   5   6
ft.

Your neighbor's
cat Al Fresco
enjoys chasing the
birds that come to
the bird bath in
your garden.

How can you make the bird bath
safe for the birds?

Try using some of these things.

roll of plastic netting:
6 ft. wide, 30 ft. long

clear plastic fish bowl

← 2 ft. →

cotton balls

feathers

tennis ball

glue

food coloring

colander

battery operated cassette player

blank cassette

hammer

← 3 ft. →

1 ft.

flexible metal sheet

nails

screws

drill

screwdriver

string

bell

eye dropper

toy mouse on wheels

alarm clock

shovel

wire spring

foil

bulb

strong scissors

copper wire

batteries

cardboard box

← 2 ft. →

13

The disaster in the fish pond

On a field trip to the zoo you dropped four things in a pond:

your uncle's brand new video camera

leaking batteries from your cassette player

your best friend's zoo project

and your lunch

- The water will ruin the camera.
- The leaking batteries will kill the fish.
- Your best friend needs her zoo project back tonight.
- You are feeling very hungry.

RARE AND ENDANGERED
ELECTRIC JUMPING FISH
WATER PURITY ESSENTIAL
ANY CONTAMINANT WILL KILL THE FISH

water lilies cover whole of pond

the rare and endangered Electric Jumping Fish (last breeding pair)

concrete lining

water weeds which are eaten by fish

fresh water

water snails which keep pool clean

your lunch

zoo project book

2 ft.

clay pipe

video camera

leaking batteries

drain to river clogged up here

Costs (in dollars)

video camera $1,000
4 batteries $3
fish   priceless
project book $5
lunch $10

You have time to save only one of four things: the camera, or the fish, or the zoo project, or your lunch.

Which one do you save?
Why and how?
This time you decide what you need.

Index